From Insanity to Serenity

A Journey from Despair to Resilience: Book of Poetry

From Insanity to Serenity

A Journey from Despair to Resilience: Book of Poetry

Poetry by

Darren C. Skinner, LSW, MSW, Ph.D.

Gotham Books

30 N Gould St.
Ste. 20820, Sheridan, WY 82801
https://gothambooksinc.com/

Phone: 1 (307) 464-7800

© 2025 *Darren C. Skinner, LSW, MSW, Ph.D*. All rights reserved.

No part of this book may be reproduced, stored in a retrieval system, or transmitted by any means without the written permission of the author.

Published by Gotham Books (May 14, 2025)

ISBN: 979-8-3493-3505-1 (H)
ISBN: 979-8-3493-3503-7 (P)
ISBN: 979-8-3493-3504-4 (E)

Because of the dynamic nature of the Internet, any web addresses or links contained in this book may have changed since publication and may no longer be valid.

The views expressed in this work are solely those of the author and do not necessarily reflect the views of the publisher, and the publisher hereby disclaims any responsibility for them.

Book Reviews

Nancy Boll

I found the poems to have a soothing lyrical sound. I enjoyed reading them, the titles were something that I connected to as I'm in recovery. The poems themselves were deeply meaningful to me as they were deep n positive.

Sunnie Majid

It's often difficult to be objective about good friends and family, but here goes. I attended a spiritual retreat last year and exchanged contact information with a retreat brother I have known for years.

Darren asked me to read a poem he had written and requested my opinion. I was very impressed and asked if it was the only poem he had written. We began texting and talking regularly, and he started sending me poems on a weekly basis. These poems, spiritual in nature, were a pleasure to read. As someone who has been reading the collected works of Robert Burns my entire life, I mention this to emphasize my love for reading.

I asked Darren if he had published any poetry, and he shared a wonderful story from his childhood. His mother had submitted one of his poems to a contest, and he won. My immediate reaction was, "You have to get published!"

Recently, Darren informed me that he is now under contract with Gotham Publishing Company. I feel very blessed to have read some of his poetry before it was published and am grateful to have observed and shared in his journey from "point A to point B." Thanks for the ride.

Robert Mann

The poems tell a story. The deliberate choice of words allowed my imagination to feel exactly what the author was describing. The poems vividly described, feeling, yet ended with a message of hope.

Kristen Hall, CEI
Vice President of Business Development
Footprints to Recovery
Aliya Health Group

I was really moved by your poems. I felt like your words took me on a spiritual ride into my own recovery journey. I felt like your words took me on a spiritual ride to into my own recovery journey. The word you choose to use gave imagery into my own experience with hitting bottom. I also appreciated how the words flowed with progression from despair to an awakening. Your poems are gentle yet impactful for one's personal, and courageous journey through life.

Thanks for sharing!

Lesa Jones
Peer Support Specialist III
University Behavioral Health Care- MWRAP Program

"From Insanity to Recovery" I've enjoyed reading the one regarding daughter's it was very moving and it touched my heart... I also loved Living in Peace and Redemption... The poems were very inspiring and I'm looking forward to reading them more more each day... They are inspirational and they lift your spirits... Thank you and I can't wait to read more more of your work...

Aurora Gonzalez-Skinner

I was privileged enough to read some pieces by Darren, and am so thrilled that he has published a whole book of them for us all! His work is powerful, yet humble. It is honest and forthright. It is sensitive and loving. And it brings us a strong message of hope in recovery from so many hardships. We are blessed to have this artist in our midst, expressing his most deep felt work with the world.

Marissa Woodrow

Simple, sweet truths set beautifully to poetry; each poem is an invitation to meditation. Truly beautiful work by Darren!!

Leslie Dameron

I was honored that Darren Skinner shared his poetry with me. His poetry resonates with those seeking personal change and inner peace, often rooted in the experience of recovery or self-reflection. Through titles like *Courage to Change*, *12 Steps of AA*, *The Quiet Mind*, and *Unspoken Words*, Skinner's work conveys a deep commitment of emotional honesty, vulnerability, and spiritual growth. His poetry speaks to the transformative journey many undergo when facing personal struggles—whether addiction, mental health, or simply the human condition.

Keith Roig

Dr. Darren Skinner's poetry is deeply personal, reflective, and aimed at those navigating complex emotional terrain. His work holds the potential to inspire, offering a voice for those struggling with change and looking for guidance or solace. Whether writing about the structured journey of AA's 12 Steps, the quiet contemplation of the mind, or the power of unspoken words, Skinner captures essential human experiences with both sensitivity and clarity. His poems would likely resonate with readers on a healing journey, providing both insight and emotional support.

Jodie Reid

This poem deeply resonates with me as it embodies courage, hope, unity, and the principle of leaving no one behind in challenging times. It powerfully illustrates that, as a nation, we may bend but will never break. Reading it brought a profound sense of sadness, yet ultimately filled me with hope as I reflected on that day. Great poems Darren!

Introduction

Welcome to *From Insanity to Serenity - A Journey from Despair to Resilience*. This collection of poetry is a reflection of my journey through darkness, turmoil, and eventually into healing, acceptance, and peace. The poems in this book capture the various stages of my personal struggle with addiction and trauma, as well as the hard-earned growth that has emerged through perseverance and recovery.

I have experienced the highs and lows, the moments of despair, and the faint glimmers of hope that eventually turned into a steady flame of resilience. Each poem is a piece of my soul, woven together with the threads of pain, hope, and transformation. Through these words, I hope to reach others who may be walking a similar path, reminding them that even in the deepest darkness, there is always a way forward.

This collection is more than just a series of poems—it is a testament to the power of self-discovery, healing, and the unwavering spirit that can arise from the ashes of addiction. I am humbled to share this with you, hoping it will inspire and resonate with anyone seeking solace, strength, and serenity.

Acknowledgments

This book would not have been possible without the support and encouragement of my loved ones, and Footprints to Recovery. My reawakening began there, and I was given another moment of grace. So, thank you to the Footprints to Recovery leadership and staff, whose dedication and faith in me, were seeds that were planted and took root and growed. Thank you! Also, I want to thank my daughters, Dawn and Shatina, for being my constant motivation and encouraging me to share my poetry with the world. Your belief in me has been a guiding light through my darkest times.

To my family and friends—Aurora S., Robert M., Sean Mc., Izzy V., and Ron B.—your support and understanding have been invaluable. Each of you has played a role in shaping this book, and I am deeply grateful. Aurora S., was my main champion and cheer leader, who always knew I had a book in me. I also want to extend my heartfelt thanks to all my friends who have read and appreciated my poetry over the years. Your words of encouragement and appreciation have given me the courage to keep writing and to compile this collection.

Lastly, I want to thank SJI, Footprints to Recovery, and my brothers and sisters in the recovery community. You have inspired me, walked beside me, and reminded me that I am never alone in this journey. It is because of the strength I've witnessed in all of you that I have found the courage to share my story.

This book is dedicated to every soul who has ever struggled in silence, and to those who are brave enough to seek a path of healing and hope.

Dedication

This book is dedicated to my belief in God, who has been my ultimate guide, strength, and purpose throughout this journey of recovery and self-discovery. To my daughters, Dawn and Shatina, who have been my light and inspiration, reminding me of the importance of resilience and love. And to Aurora Skinner, who has encouraged me for years to put my words on paper and turn my journey into something to be shared.

To the New York City Public Library, where in 1992, I began this creative journey and discovered the power of words as a means of healing and expression.

To my grandmother, Grace, who instilled in me a lifelong love and value for education, and whose wisdom and encouragement have shaped me profoundly.

To the mentors and colleagues who, since 2011, inspired me to start collecting my poetry and gave me the courage to believe it was worth sharing.

To St. Joseph's Institute for Addictions and Footprints to Recovery – the organizations that provided me a safe place to rediscover myself mentally, physically, and spiritually.

Special thanks to Emily Benjamin, Kristen Hall, and Lisa Fobian, who saw potential in me, even when I couldn't see it in myself.

To all the men and women in and around Princeton, NJ, who have embraced, supported, and loved me through every stage of my recovery journey (you know who you are). Especially people like Ron Boll, Sean McShane, Robert Mann, and countless others. Without each of you, my path would look very different. Thank you for believing in me and for being part of this journey.

Table of Contents

Book Reviews v
Introduction ix
Acknowledgments x
Dedication xii
Conclusion xviii
Chapter I: Despair and Struggle 1
    The Fractured Mind 1
    The Effects of Trauma 2
    Loneliness 3
    Through the Storm 4
    The Silent Keeper 4
Chapter II: Reflection and Recovery 6
    Sobriety and Recovery 6
    Faith 7
    Gratitude 8
    Hope 8
    Trust 9
    Spirituality 10
    Redemption 10
Chapter III: Transformation and Healing 12
    The Power of Now 12

The Quiet Mind 13

The Gift of Acceptance...14

The Path Unseen 15

Mindfulness 16

Thank God for AA..16

Chapter IV: Resilience and Strength 18

The Steady Calm 18

Thriving, Not Surviving 19

Live in Peace 20

The Gift of Grace...20

Threads of Light 21

The Power of Words 22

A Path of Twelve 23

Chapter V: Love and Connection..25

The Cool 25

The Light 25

I Know What I Want..25

I Sleep Well..26

A New Light in My Life..27

Beyond Assumptions 29

The Best You Give...30

Chapter VI: Acceptance and Serenity 32

The Dance of Two 32

A Mother's Love..33

    The Shield Within 34

    Let's Be Kind 35

    Endless Currents 35

Chapter VII: Spiritual Awakening 37

    The Universe is Calling 37

    God's Grace 38

    The Courage to Change 38

    Religious or Spiritual? 39

    A God Wink 40

Chapter VIII: Love and Connection 42

    The Essence of Love 42

    The Dance of Two 43

    When Cupid Aimed His Arrow 44

    My Darling Daughter 44

    The Unspoken Words 45

    What Is Love? 46

Chapter IX: Growth and Healing 48

    Hope in Healing 48

    Raise Your Level of Consciousness 49

    Authentic Self 50

    Please Help Me Heal 51

    My Inner Child 52

    Footprints to Recovery 53

Chapter X: When I Open My Eyes 54
    The Strength in Surrender: 54
    The Foundation of H.O.W. 55
    No More Drama 56
    Is it a Butterfly, a Bird, or an Angel? 57
    Alone in the Universe 58
    Making Peace with One's Past 59
    Wake Up, You're in the Dark 59
    I Have a Voice 61
    Redemption 62
    When I Was Young 63
    "Remember me, for I am you." 65
    What Is Love? 66
    Note to Self 67
    I Am 69
    Blind Faith 70
    9/11: We Will Never Forget 72
    Dr. Darren C. Skinner: A Journey from Despair to Resilience 74

Conclusion

This collection of poems is a testament to the journey from despair to resilience, a reflection of the highs and lows that come with the path of recovery and self-discovery. Each piece in this book represented a step taken, a moment of God's grace, a moment of courage, and a reminder that healing is not linear, but a continuous process of growth and transformation.

As you close this book, I hope these words leave you with a sense of hope and strength. May you find comfort in knowing that no matter how dark the path may seem, there is always light, always a way forward.

Thank you for taking the time to walk through this journey with me. I am forever grateful for your support, and I hope these poems inspire and resonate with you, just as they have been a source of healing and understanding for me.

Chapter I:
Despair and Struggle

The Fractured Mind

A whisper in the silent night, a flicker of a distant light, reality bends, begins to sway, as reason slowly slips away. The mind, once clear, now twists and turns, a fire within that never burns, voices echo, shadows play, in corners where the sane would stray.

The world is skewed, a mirrored maze, trapped in a fog, in endless haze, where thoughts collide, and visions blend, and every start has lost its end. A constant loop, a broken reel, where nothing's true, yet all feels real, emotions spiral, dark and wild, a storm within the tortured child.

Clinging tight to fleeting strands, of reason's grasp with trembling hands, but every tether snaps in two, as madness paints its vivid hue. The laughter, hollow, rings like bells, in empty halls where silence dwells, and every face, a stranger's mask, hiding truths too dark to ask.

Is it a dream, or is it real? This fractured world, this surreal feel, where sense is lost, and chaos reigns, and sanity unravels its chains. Yet in the depths, a plea, a cry, a hope that someday it will die, the madness, the wild, relentless sea, and set the fractured spirit free.

But until then, the mind will roam, in twisted paths, far from home, a place where reason dares not tread, in the labyrinth of the living dead.

The Effects of Trauma

Trauma is the shadow that lingers near, a silent echo of pain and fear. It's the wound that hides beneath the skin, a battle fought, but not yet won within.

It's the nights when sleep won't come, the racing thoughts that leave us numb. Trauma is the weight that bends the spine, the silent scream that we call "mine."

It's the trust that falters, the heart that aches, the piece of joy that trauma takes. It's the flash of memory, sharp and cold, the story untold, but always told.

Trauma is the fear that grips the soul, a thief of peace, a broken whole. It's the tears that fall without a sound, the heavy heart, the battleground.

But trauma is also the fight to heal, the journey to feel what we once could feel. It's the courage to face what we have known, to reclaim our lives, to be our own.

The effects of trauma, deep and wide, but within us all, the strength to rise. For every wound, there is a scar, a testament to how strong we are.

In the midst of pain, we seek the light, in the darkest hour, we find our might. For though trauma leaves its mark, within us all, there is a spark. A hope that one day we will be free, to live, to love, to simply be. For in the end, though trauma stays, we learn to heal in our own way.

Loneliness

Loneliness is the empty room, a silent echo, a heavy gloom. It's the space where voices fade, the quiet shadow where hearts are weighed. It's the feeling of being lost in a crowd, a muffled cry, not spoken aloud. Loneliness is the cold in the chest, a restless soul that cannot rest.

It's the long night with no end in sight, the search for warmth, the absence of light. Loneliness is the tear unshed, the heavy heart, the sinking dread. It's the empty chair, the unmade bed, the quiet thoughts that fill your head. Loneliness is the reaching hand, that finds no grasp, no place to land.

But loneliness is also the chance to see, the depths within, the strength to be. It's the moment to pause, to reflect, to grow, to find yourself when the world feels slow. In the quiet, there's a voice that speaks, a truth that's found when the heart is weak.

For loneliness, though hard to bear, It's the path that leads to self-aware.

So while loneliness may come and stay, it also has the power to lead the way, to deeper love, to truer friends, to the healing that begins when loneliness ends.

Through the Storm

In the depths where shadows reign, a heart weighed down by silent pain, trauma whispers, etched in scars, a past that left a world ajar. Eyes once clouded, lost in haze, where every step felt like a maze, but through the dark, a flicker came, a sober light, a whispering flame.

Mental storms, relentless tide, waves of doubt that never died, yet in the turmoil, strength was found, in sober breath, on solid ground. To heal the wounds that time forgot, to face the pain that truth has brought, is to unearth what's buried deep, and in the open, freely weep.

But every tear, a cleansing rain, washes away the silent pain, and in the calm that follows near, a peace emerges, crystal clear. For in sobriety, there's space to heal, to let the mind and spirit feel, the weight of trauma, softening slow, As the seeds of self-compassion grow.

So, to the soul that seeks the light, In the darkest hour of the night, know that in the pain you bear, a path to healing lies somewhere. And with each step, though small it be, you'll find your way to being free, for in the journey to be whole, you'll find the courage in your soul.

The Silent Keeper

Time, the silent keeper's hand, marks each moment, like a grain of sand, a river flowing, ever swift, from dawn's first light to twilight's drift. It ticks away in steady beat, in every breath, in every feat, a constant pulse, unseen, unheard, yet felt in every passing word.

Time, a thief in daylight's glow, steals the moment, fast or slow, a fleeting glance, a tender kiss, each one a memory we miss. It carves the lines upon our face, a gentle, yet relentless trace, of every joy, of every tear, a witness to each passing year.

Time, the teacher, wise and old, reveals the truths that life has told, in every lesson, every scar, it shapes the person that we are. It heals the wounds, it mends the heart, yet also tears our world apart, a paradox of loss and gain, of fleeting peace, of lingering pain.

Time, a gift we often waste, in endless hurry, endless haste, yet in its depths, there lies a key, to live, to love, to simply be. For in the now, where time stands still, we find the strength, we find the will, to savor every fleeting hour, and harness time's enduring power. So, cherish time, this precious thread, for once it's gone, consider it dead.

Chapter II:
Reflection and Recovery

Sobriety and Recovery

Sobriety is the dawn after a long, dark night, a step toward the sun, from shadows and fright. It's the first breath of air, clean and pure, a promise to oneself that life will endure.

Recovery is the path where hope is found, a journey of healing, where we turn around. It's the courage to face what once was ignored, the strength to rebuild what's been shattered and torn.

In sobriety, the mind finds peace, a release from the chains that once did seize. It's the clarity that washes the soul, a steady climb toward being whole.

Recovery is the hand that reaches within, to mend the heart and heal the sin. It's the light that guides through the darkest days, a beacon of hope in life's tangled maze.

Self-help is the compass that points the way, a guide that whispers, "You'll be okay." It's the wisdom found in the quietest places, the power to rise, to meet life's graces.

In sobriety, we reclaim our name, in recovery, we rise from the flame.

Self-help is the thread that binds it all, a reminder that even in darkness, we stand tall.

So, walk the path with a steady stride, in sobriety and recovery, let love be your guide. For in every step, in every choice, there's a quiet victory, a strengthened voice.

The road is long, but you're not alone, in the journey of self, you've always grown. With each breath, you find the way, in sobriety and recovery, you'll never stray.

Faith

Faith is a whisper in the darkest night, a spark that flickers yet holds on tight. It's the strength to step when the path is unclear, a gentle voice that says, "I am near."

It's the trust in the dawn after a long, cold rain, the belief in growth through every pain. It's the light that shines through doubt and fear, the courage to stand when no one is near.

Faith is a bridge when the waters rise, a steady gaze that defies the skies. It's the hope that blooms in barren ground, a silent song with a powerful sound.

In every heart, faith finds its home, guiding the star wherever we roam. Through every trial, with love as our guide, faith walks beside us, stride for stride.

Gratitude

Gratitude is the sunrise in a clear morning sky, a quiet whisper of thanks echoes high. It's the warmth in our hearts when the day is done, the peace in our soul when battles are won.

It's the smile we give without a thought, the joy in knowing how far we've sought. Gratitude is the gentle rain on thirsty earth, a reminder of love, of endless worth.

It's the light that glows in simple things, In the song that every moment sings. Gratitude is the hand we hold, the stories shared; the memories told.

In every breath, in every beat, gratitude makes our lives complete. It's the key that opens the door to grace, a tender touch, an embrace. So let our hearts be full, our spirits rise, with gratitude shining in our eyes. For every blessing, great and small, gratitude is the greatest gift of all.

Hope

Hope is the star in a stormy sky, a beacon that gleams as the night draws nigh. It's the promise of dawn after endless night, the quiet belief that wrongs will be right.

It's the breath we take when the world feels tight, the courage to push through the darkest plight. Hope is the seed in the barren ground, the whisper of life when no life is found. It's the wings of a bird on its first flight, the steady flame that refuses to die. Hope is the bridge that spans despair, a gentle breeze in the stifling air.

In the hearts of the weary, hope takes hold, a story of tomorrow yet to be told.

It's the faith that blooms in the face of strife, the heartbeat of a better life. So let hope rise like a golden sun, a light that shines for everyone. For in hope, we find the strength to cope, and in its warmth, we are forever aglow.

Trust

Trust is a fragile, yet powerful thread, a bond of gold where fears are shed.

It's the hand you hold in the darkest of days, a silent pact in countless ways.

It's the leap of faith when the ground's unsure, a knowing heart that love will endure. Trust is the bridge that closes the gap, a steadfast anchor, a gentle map.

It's the gaze that holds without a doubt, the steady light when all seems out. Trust is the soil where friendships grow, a sacred space where we can show our deepest thoughts, our hidden scars, and find acceptance in each other's arms.

In every promise, trust takes flight, a beacon that guides us through the night. It's the quiet strength, the unspoken vow, the peace in knowing, here and now.

So, guard it well, but give it free, for trust is the key to harmony. In every heart, let trust be found, a precious gift, ever profound.

Spirituality

Spirituality is the breath between breaths, a whisper of truth where the soul connects. It's the silence that speaks in the quiet of dawn, a sacred dance where the self is drawn.

It's the light that shines from deep within, a journey of seeking where we begin. Spirituality is the wind in the trees, the song of the earth, the voice of the seas.

It's the stillness found in a restless mind, a gentle embrace, both tender and kind. It's the thread that weaves through every heart, a reminder that we are all a part.

In every prayer, in every sigh, spirituality is the reason why. Where we search for meaning beyond the seen, in the spaces where the heart is keen.

It's the faith in something greater than we, a path of light where the soul runs free. Spirituality is the star above, a call to peace, a call to love. So let your spirit rise and soar, to the heights where truth is more. In every moment, seek the divine, for spirituality is where we align.

Redemption

Through shadows deep, I walked alone, with heavy heart, a soul of stone. Each step I took, a path of wrong, lost in darkness far too long.

But in the quiet, through the night,

A flicker grew, a gentle light.

A voice within began to call,

To rise again, though I may fall.

Redemption's hand, it reached for me, a promise whispered, "You are free." Not in perfection, but in grace,

I found my way, my rightful place. In brokenness, I found my strength,

Through every trial, I went the length.

Forgiveness bloomed, a second chance, to heal, to grow, to learn the dance. now, with each day, I rise anew, with scars as proof of what I knew:

That even from the depths of pain, Redemption waits, like soft, warm rain.

Chapter III:
Transformation and Healing

The Power of Now

In the rush of time, where moments blur, and dreams of past and future stir, there lies a space, a quiet vow, a sacred place: the power of now. The past, a shadow, long and wide, the future, waves that push and chide, but here, in this breath, this fleeting beat, is where our hearts and spirits meet.

 No more regrets, no anxious dread, no weight of words left unsaid, for in the now, we find release, a tender calm, a perfect peace. Each breath a gift, each moment pure, a present truth that will endure, beyond the bounds of time and fear, the power of now is always near.

To live, to love, and to fully be; to see the world with clarity... no yesterday, no tomorrow's call, just the present, where we stand tall. In this moment, all is clear, the sounds, the sights, the feelings dear, for when we stay, when we allow, we find our strength in the power of now.

No need to chase what lies ahead, or cling to what's been done or said, for life unfolds in the here and now, a gentle truth, a simple vow. So breathe it in, let go, be free, the power of now is all you need, to find your way, to live, to grow, in this moment, let your spirit flow.

The Quiet Mind

In the stillness of the morning light, when the world is soft, and day is bright, there lies a space, calm and kind, a gentle place within the mind. Mindfulness, a tender art, to be, to see, with an open heart, no rush, no worry, no endless chase, just a moment's peace, a sacred grace.

Each breath, a whisper, soft and true, each thought, a cloud that drifts in view, no clinging tight, no pushing away, just letting be what comes your way. The past can wait, the future too, for in this moment, it's just you, with eyes that see, with ears that hear, the simple joys that linger near. The rustling leaves, the softest breeze, the songs of birds among the trees, in mindful steps, you walk the earth, in every sound, you find its worth.

To taste, to touch, to truly feel, the things that make this life so real, with a mindful heart, with a quiet grace, you will find your soul in every place. No need to judge, no need to fight, just be the witness to your light, in mindfulness, you come to see, the beauty in simplicity.

For in this practice, soft and slow, you learn to let the old wounds go, to live, to love, in the here and now, to honor life, to take a vow. To be aware, to truly know, the power in the present flow, Mindfulness, a gentle guide, to walk with peace, with truth inside.

The Gift of Acceptance

In the tangled web of life's embrace,

Where troubles seem to fill each space, I searched for answers, sought control, to ease the weight upon my soul. But in the fight, the push, the pull, the more I grasped, the less felt full, until one day, I came to see, that peace was in accepting me.

Acceptance, soft as morning's light,

A gentle hand that holds me tight,

It whispers, "Let go, just be still,

and trust the flow, the greater will. "For every storm that shakes my core, there's calm in knowing, nothing more, that life unfolds, in ways unknown, and in that truth, I'm not alone.

Acceptance isn't giving in, it's not a loss, nor is it sin, it's finding strength in letting be, in trusting what I cannot see. The problems that once seemed so tall, now crumble, fade, become so small, for in accepting what I face, I find within a quiet grace.

No need to fix what's out of hand,

No need to force what I can't stand,

For when I welcome what's in sight,

The weight I carried turns to light. In every challenge, every test,

acceptance leads me to my best,

a key to peace, to setting free,

The tangled knots inside of me.

So here I stand, with open heart,

Embracing life in every part, for in acceptance, I have found, the truest peace, the solid ground.

The Path Unseen

With eyes closed tight, I walk the way, through shadows deep, through skies of gray, no map in hand, no light to guide, just faith alone, where doubts reside. Blind faith, they call it, strong and pure, a trust in things that are unsure, a leap into the great unknown, where reason falters, truth is shown.

It's not in facts, or what we see,

But in a hope that sets us free,

A quiet voice that whispers near,

"Keep going, love, you need not fear. "For blind faith walks where sight can't tread, a journey led by heart instead, through winding roads and rocky climbs, It trusts in life, it trusts in time.

No need to know the why, the how,

Simply place your hand upon the plow,

And with each step, though steep the hill, blind faith will guide your steadfast will. The world may scoff, the winds may blow, yet through it all, the heart will know, that though unseen, the path is right, for blind faith walks with inner light.

And when you stand upon the peak,

With every answer that you seek,

You'll find it wasn't sight or plan,

But trust in things beyond what man. For faith, though blind, will see you through, when all seems lost, and doubt is due, it's in the leap, the step you take, that faith's true vision will awake.

Mindfulness

In the quiet space between each thought, where time slows down and seems caught, there lives a peace, both calm and clear, a presence that whispers, "I am here."

Each breath a gift, each moment pure, a fleeting second, we are sure.

The world may spin, the storms may rage, but mindfulness turns a soothing page.

Notice the rain, the wind, the sky, the gentle flutter of a butterfly. Each beat of the heart, each sigh of the air, a reminder that we are fully aware.

No future worries, no past regret, just this moment where all is set.

In mindfulness, we simply are, we be, awake, alive, and truly free.

Thank God for AA

To AA, my heart extends its praise, for guiding me through the darkest days. When shadows clung, and hope was small, you lifted me and stilled my fall.

With open arms and steady grace, you gave me strength to find my place. Each step, a path to heal and grow, in rooms of wisdom, love would flow.

Through shared experiences, bonds were made, with hands held tight, I wasn't afraid. The burdens shared, the weights released, my soul began to find its peace.

And so I thank the ones who came, who walk this road and know my name. Together, we are strong and basically the same, In fellowship we survive the day to day pain.

In helping others, it helps us too, to stay true to our purpose and spiritually renew.

So, thank God for AA, a path divine, through faith and hope we grow one day at a time, thy will be done not mine.

Chapter IV:
Resilience and Strength

The Steady Calm

In the quiet hours before the dawn, when shadows linger, and hope seems gone, a trembling heart, once drowned in drink, begins to rise, begins to think. No longer numb, no longer blind, the storm within, a restless mind, now seeks a path, a steady way, to face the truth of every day.

Emotional sobriety, a tender grace, found in each breath, in each small space, where feelings stir, no longer chained, by the liquid lies that once explained.

The highs, the lows, the endless fight, the longing for that fleeting light, now grounded in a deeper peace, where the need for more begins to cease.

To feel the pain and not to run, to face the fear, to let it come, is to embrace the waves that crash, without the bottle's bitter ash. In this journey, slow but sure, the wounds of old begin to cure, as clarity becomes the guide, and truth walks steady by your side.

Emotional sobriety, a fragile bloom, growing strong in the light of the room, where shadows fall, but do not stay, for the heart has found a brighter way. No longer lost in yesterday's tears, no longer held by forgotten fears, in the calm that only truth can bring, a sober heart begins to sing.

And in that song, a strength is born, a peace that greets each morning's dawn, for in this life, raw and real, the power of sobriety is to feel.

Thriving, Not Surviving

I am not here just to survive, to merely exist, to barely strive. I am here to thrive, to soar, to shine, to claim this life and make it mine. Surviving is a fight to breathe, a struggle to stand, to never leave.

But thriving is dancing in the rain, embracing joy, releasing pain. It's waking up with purpose clear, with strength in heart and vision near.

It's rising above the scars and fear, to live each day with passion dear. Thriving is the fire in the soul, the hunger for more, the reaching goal. It's the dream that pushes through the night, the courage to stand and fight.

No longer content just to get by, I spread my wings, I learn to fly.

For thriving is where true life begins, where every loss turns into wins.

It's the laughter that echoes loud, the confidence to stand out in a crowd. It's the love that flows, the joy that stays, the gratitude that fills my days.

So I choose to thrive, to live fully and free, to embrace all the beauty that's meant for me. I'm not just surviving, I'm alive, and in this life, I choose to thrive.

Live in Peace

In the quiet of dawn, let your heart be still, let go of the weight that bends your will. For in the soft whisper of nature's song, you'll find a place where you truly belong.

Live in peace, let the storms subside, in the depths of calm, let your soul reside. The battles we fight, the wars we wage, are merely echoes of an ancient rage.

But peace is born in a tender breath,

In a love that spans beyond life and death. It's in the smiles we share, the hands we hold, in kindness, more precious than silver or gold.

So walk in the light, let hatred cease,

And sow the seeds of lasting peace.

For when hearts unite, when love's flame is fanned, peace will blossom across the land.

The Gift of Grace

I wandered long in the shadows deep, my heart adrift, no peace to keep. The world is a maze, a twisted thread, no path ahead, just doubts instead.

But then, a light, a whispered sound. In gentle hands, my soul was found. Another chance, a moment rare, a breath of grace, beyond compare. No longer lost in endless night, I walk with purpose in the light.

This gift of time, I hold so dear

No more to waste, no more to fear. With open eyes, I face the dawn, a second chance to carry on. For in this grace, I find my place, a life renewed, a boundless space.

Threads of Light

In a world vast and wide, we roam, seeking solace, seeking home, through valleys deep and mountains high, underneath a shared sky. Alone, we tremble in the night, but together, we are threads of light, woven tight, hand in hand, we form a tapestry across the land.

A whispered word, a gentle touch, in simple things, it means so much, the power of a friendly smile, can bridge the longest, hardest mile. In another's eyes, we find our place, a mirrored soul, a kindred face, through every laugh, through every tear, the strength of connection draws us near.

It heals the wounds that life may bring, it lifts the heart and makes it sing, in times of joy, in times of strife, connection is the thread of life. From heart to heart, from soul to soul, it makes us human, makes us whole, a bond unseen, yet ever strong, a melody, a sacred song.

For in each other, we discover, the warmth of friend, the love of lover, a light that never fades away, but grows with each and every day. So cherish every bond you make, for in those ties, the world will wake, to the truth that in connection's glow, we find the strength to heal, to grow.

The Power of Words

In every word we choose to speak, lies a power vast, profound, unique, a force that shapes, that builds, that breaks, a gift we give, or trust we take. To be impeccable with what we say, is to honor truth in every way, to let our words be pure and clear, to speak with love, to speak with care.

For words, once spoken, cannot return, they linger, echo, twist, and burn, or they can heal, uplift, and mend, a bridge to foe, or bond to friend. So choose with thought, let silence be, a place where wisdom flows so free, for in the pause before we speak, we find the strength to be unique.

To speak with kindness, gentle and true, to say what's right, what's fair, what's due, is to respect the hearts we touch, to honor life, and love so much. Impeccable in word and deed, we plant a strong, enduring seed, of trust, of peace, of light that shines, in every spoken, thoughtful line.

No need to boast, no need to tear, for in our words, we show we care, and with each truth, we pave the way, for brighter, better, kinder days. So let your words be pure and bright, a beacon in the darkest night, for in this world, both vast and small, impeccable words can heal us all.

A Path of Twelve

In the darkness where I once did stray, lost in shadows, night and day, a beacon called, a steady light, a path of twelve to guide me right. Step by step, the journey starts, a reckoning within my heart, to face the truth, to make amends, to find a way where healing begins.

First, I yielded, bowed my head, admitted where my soul soon bled, powerless before the fight, surrendered to a higher might. With open eyes, I searched my past, unveiling truths long overcast, a moral inventory, raw and real, each scar, each wound, began to heal.

Confession flowed, a gentle tide, no longer had I needed to hide, with every word, a burden lifts, releasing pain through honest gifts. Ready now to change my ways, to seek the light in darker days, I asked for strength, for courage too, to live a life both pure and true.

Amends I made to those I wronged, a healing thread that grew prolonged, for in each step, I found release, a closer walk toward inner peace. Through prayer, through silence, deep and still, I sought the wisdom of the will, to know what's right, to find the grace.

To walk this earth with a sober pace. And as I walked, I reached a hand, to others lost across the land, for in the giving, I receive, a truth that helps my soul believe.

The twelve steps etched within my heart, a guide for living, a brand-new start, not just for life, but every day, a spiritual path showing me the way. For in these steps, a mind reborn, with every dawn, a brand-new morn, a way to live, to rise, to strive, to believe in me, and embrace this gift called sobriety.

Chapter V:
Love and Connection

The Cool

Summer's heat, a heavy sigh, humidity clings, a sticky sky.

But it's calm, a steady breeze, a cool sunshine, if you please.

Her laughter, ice to melt the day, a refreshing shade, a vibrant ray.

With her around, the world's alright, a cooling comfort, shining bright.

The Light

A gem, a radiant spark, a shining beacon, reaching far. The beauty blooms, a graceful art, a warmth that mends the wounded heart.

Like sunlight dancing on the sea, the spirit shines, wild and free. A brilliant light, a sight so deep, its blinding, it's bright, that memory I'll keep.

I Know What I Want

In the quiet moments of the night, when the world is still, and stars are bright. A whisper stirs within my mind, a truth so clear, I've come to find. I know what I want, and it's you, your name a melody, a sweet sonata. In every thought, you linger near, a new constant presence, ever so dear.

From dawn's first light to twilight's hue, my heart sings softly, "It's you, it's you." In dreams you dance, a vision sweet, in waking hours, my soul you meet.

The world fades to a distant blur, when I think of you, my hearts astir. Your laughter, I imagine your smile, your gentle grace, in my life, you hold a cherished place.

I know what I want, and it's you. A potential love can be true. With every beat, my heart aligns, to the rhythm of your name, divine.

So here I stand, my feelings clear, a connection that's strong, a potential love that's nearby. I know what I want, and it's you, for in my thoughts, it's you I treasure, a potential future, together we'll find the sweetest pleasure.

I Sleep Well

In the quiet of the night, stars softly gleam, your name is a whisper, a sweet, gentle theme. In the twilight, where dream softly tread I sleep well, when, before going to bed, I'm thinking of you.

Moonlight spills silver on the world so still, a canvas of peace, where heartstrings fulfill. Your laughter, a melody, in memories embedded, I sleep well, when, before going to bed, I'm thinking of you.

Through the silence, your voice echoes clear, a symphony of comfort, drawing you nearby. In the embrace of darkness, dreams are threaded, I sleep well, when, before going to bed, I'm thinking of you.

With each thought of you, the night's shadows fade, love's tender touch in the moonlight displayed. Your presence a balm, my spirit is steadied, I sleep well, when, before going to bed, I'm thinking of you.

In dreams, we wander through fields of delight, hand in hand, beneath the stars so bright.

In the cradle of night, my soul is embedded, I sleep well, when, before going to bed, I'm thinking of you.

A New Light in My Life

In the quiet moments of doubt and fear, your words find me, soft and sincere.

A gentle push, a caring hand, you guide me through this uncertain land.

With kindness woven into every phrase, you lift me up and set my spirit ablaze.

Your friendship, a beacon in the night, brings hope and strength, pure delight.

I never knew how much I'd need, a soul like yours, to plant the seed,

of dreams and hopes, of something more, a bright future, an open door.

You're the force I didn't see, but now I'm sure you're meant for me.

Inspiring, kind, and always near, with you, there's nothing left to fear.

And as we walk this path of friends, I can't help but hope it never ends.

For in my heart, a wish does start, that one day, we'll share a deeper part.

Beyond Assumptions

In the quiet spaces of the mind,

Where thoughts like whispers intertwine, we often build what's not quite true, assumptions shaping what we view. A glance, a word, a fleeting tone, becomes a story all our own, we fill the gaps, connect the threads, of things unsaid, of looks unread.

Yet in the tales we weave, we often misconceive and believe, we often misconceive, believe, that what we think is clear and known, is something more than what is shown. For truth is found in honest light, not in the shadows of our sight, and when we ask instead of guess, we ease our hearts from needless stress.

To pause, to wait, to ask, to know,

Is to let understanding grow, to see with eyes unclouded, clear, and chase away each subtle fear. Assumptions build a fragile wall,

That keeps us distant, makes us small, but when we choose to break them down, we wear compassion as a crown.

For everyone, a story hides, that can't be seen from just outside,

And only when we dare to seek,

Do we find truths both strong and meek. So let us not assume or guess, but lean into the humbleness, of asking what is truly there, with open hearts, with mindful care.

In this, we find a world more wide,

Where understanding is our guide,

From Sanity to Serenity | 29

And in its glow, assumptions cease,

Replaced with trust, replaced with peace.

The Best You Give

In every moment, every day,

A choice is made, a certain way,

To give your all, to stand and strive,

To keep your dreams and hopes alive. Your best may vary, rise or fall,

In times of triumph, or when you stall, but what you give, from heart and soul, is what will make your spirit whole.

Some days are bright, some filled with doubt, but giving up is not the route, for when you try, though skies are gray, you'll find your strength along the way. Your best is not a perfect line, it ebbs and flows, through space and time, it's in the effort that you bring, that turns the ordinary into a spring.

It's not the prize, it's not the gain,

It's in the learning through the strain,

It's in the way you rise again, that shows your best in loss or win. So do your best, in all you do, in every task you see it through, for in the doing, there's a grace, a quiet joy, a steady pace.

And when the night falls soft and still, you'll find a peace, a deeper will, for in your best, no matter small, you've answered to your higher call. In every effort, large or slight, you shine your truth, you share your light, and though the road is never straight, your best is what will shape your fate.

Chapter VI:
Acceptance and Serenity

The Dance of Two

A man and woman, hand in hand, two souls that journey through this land, in love's embrace, they find their way, through night and dawn, through every day. Their hearts, they beat in steady rhyme, through seasons' change, through tests of time, they laugh, they cry, they learn, they grow, in every high, in every low.

At times, they dance in perfect sync, in rhythm's sway, on passion's brink, while other times, they walk alone, each needing space, each needing home. They face the storms that life may send, but find their strength when they defend, the bond they share, both fierce and kind, a love that's patient, love that's blind.

In whispered words or silent gaze, they write their story through the days, a tale of joy, of trials too, of finding self, yet being two. For in the woman's tender heart, the man finds shelter, finds his part, and in the man's strong, steady hand, the woman feels her spirit stand.

Yet more than love, it's trust they build, a quiet peace that's softly filled, with moments small, yet deeply true, a partnership that sees them through. It's in the give, it's in the take, the compromises that they make, for love is not just wild desire, but steady warmth, a constant fire.

So man and woman walk this life, as friends, as lovers, husband, wife, in union strong, in gentle grace, together in this sacred space.

A Mother's Love

In your embrace, I found my start, the beating of your tender heart, a rhythm that has guided me, through all of life's vast, stormy sea. Your hands, so gentle, yet so strong, have led me right when I was wrong, with every touch, a soothing balm, a shelter in the fiercest calm. Your voice, a melody so sweet, a comfort in the dark's retreat, It lifted me when I was low, a constant light, a steady glow.

Through every joy and every tear, your love was always ever near, a lighthouse on the roughest shore, that held me close, that loved me more. Your wisdom, in each word you said, a compass when I lost my head, you taught me how to stand and fight, and when to yield, when to fight.

In all you gave, you asked no gain, you bore the weight of joy and pain, for in your heart, a love so deep, it carries me, in waking, sleep. I see your strength, I see your grace, in every line upon your face, a testament to all you've done, a life of love for daughter, son.

And though the years may pass us by, in every laugh, in every sigh, I'll carry you within my soul, for you have made my spirit whole. So here's to you, my guiding star, no matter where, no matter how far, your love, my mother, pure and true, is in my heart, forever you.

The Shield Within

In a world where words can wound, and actions feel like arrows strewn, it's easy to let hurt reside, to take it in, to let it slide. But there's a wisdom deep and strong, a truth that helps us move along, to know that not all words are true, and not all actions speak of you.

For in the hearts of those who speak lies their own struggles and peaks and what they say or do, you see, is more about them, less about me. So, when the world seems harsh and cold, and words of others seem so bold, remember, you are not the source, of every slight, of every course.

To take things personally is to bear a weight that's neither fair nor square, it ties your heart in needless knots, and plants in you self-doubting thoughts. But if you let those arrows fall, if you rise above it all, you find a peace that's pure and true, a strength that comes from knowing you.

For you are not what others say, nor are you shaped by their dismay, you hold within your heart the key, to stand with grace, to just let be. So, let their words be as the breeze, that passes by with subtle ease, and in your soul, let calmness grow, for you decide what seeds to sow.

In not taking things to heart, you find the space to play your part, with open mind and spirit free, to live in peace, to simply be.

Let's Be Kind

In a world that rushes, fast and loud, where every face is lost in the crowd, there's a simple truth we often find, the greatest gift is to be kind. Let's be kind, in word and deed, to every soul, to every need, for kindness grows in hearts that care, in every smile, in every share.

A gentle word, a helping hand, can turn the tide, can change the land, for in each act, both big and small, we lift each other when we fall. Let's be kind, and take the time, to listen close, to see the sign, of those who struggle, those who hide, their pain behind a silent tide.

For kindness is the bridge we build, a light that shines when hearts are stilled, It's in the laughter that we share, in showing someone that we care. Let's be kind, for life is brief, a fleeting moment, joy and grief, and in this dance of night and day, kindness is the gentle way.

So let's be kind, in all we do, to those we love, to strangers too, for in the end, what we will find, is that the world needs us to be kind.

Endless Currents

In your eyes, I find a home, a place where time bends and slows, with every glance, a world unfolds, a love that deepens, never grows old. Your laughter, like a gentle breeze, whispers comfort, puts my heart at ease. Through every storm, through every tide, you've been the anchor at my side.

Hand in hand, we face the years, together in joy, together in tears. In your embrace, I am complete, in your love, I find my feet. No distance can dim this fire's glow, no time can erode the bond we know. For you are my heart, my soul, my light, the love that guides me through the night.

Each day with you is a gift I hold, a story of us, forever told. With you, my partner, my love, my friend, together we'll dance until the end.

Chapter VII:
Spiritual Awakening

The Universe is Calling

The universe is calling, soft and low, through starry skies and moonlit glow.

In whispered winds and cosmic streams, it pulls me closer to my dreams.

A voice within the endless night, a beacon in the distant light, it asks me now to spread my wings, to seek the truth that freedom brings.

Through galaxies that swirl and spin, it beckons me to look within. For every star that lights the sky, reminds me how to truly fly. The universe is calling clear, with songs that only hearts can hear. A symphony of boundless space, a dance with time, a cosmic grace. It calls me forth, it calls me home, in every atom, every stone.

A gentle nudge, a guiding hand, to help me rise, to help me stand. And though the path is vast and wide, with the universe, I will confide, for in its voice, I hear my name, and know I'll never be the same.

God's Grace

God's grace is the light in the darkest hour, a gentle touch, a healing power. It's the love that flows without condition, a gift so pure, beyond all tradition.

It's the hand that lifts when we have fallen, a quiet voice when the world is calling'. God's grace is the shelter in life's fierce storm, a warmth that holds, a peace that forms.

It's the strength to forgive, the courage to heal, a love so deep, so tender, so real. God's grace is the path when we've lost our way, the dawn that breaks after a weary day.

In every heart, His grace resides, a beacon of hope that gently guides. It's the light that shines through every tear, the whisper of love that calms each fear.

God's grace is the well that never runs dry, a source of life, a gentle sigh. It's the peace that settles in troubled minds, a love that heals, a love that binds.

So, trust in His grace, let it fill your soul, for in God's grace, we are made whole. It's the promise that we are never alone, in His grace, we find our home.

The Courage to Change

Beneath the surface, deep inside, where fears and doubts so often hide, a voice whispers, soft yet strong, "Find the courage to right the wrong." Change is daunting, a fearsome tide, it asks us to cast our past aside, to step away from what we know, and trust in where new winds may blow. But courage blooms in quiet places,

In hearts that dare to lift their faces, to the unknown, to the new, to the challenge of a different view. It takes a spark, a steady flame, to face the mirror, to take the blame, to say, "I'll change, I'll start anew," and follow through with what is true.

The road ahead may twist and turn, with lessons hard, and bridges burned, but in each step, in every stride, the courage to change becomes our guide. To let go of the chains that bind, and free the heart, free the mind, to trust the path, though it seems strange, this is the courage to embrace change.

In the breaking, in the bend, in the places where we mend, we find the strength, the light within, to let the new day's hope begin. For change is life, and life is change, a constant shift, a wide range, and those who dare to face the unknown, find the seeds of courage they have sown. So take the step, embrace the call, stand up strong, even if you fall, for in the trying, in the brave, we find the courage that we crave.

Religious or Spiritual?

In sacred halls where candles burn, where faithful hearts in reverence turn, the hymns of old, the prayers Intoned, a pathway carved, a faith enthroned. Religion stands, a structured way, a guiding light, a place to pray, a doctrine clear, a law defined, a bridge to where the soul may find.

But in the quiet of the night, where stars above cast gentle light, a spirit stirs, a whisper clear, beyond the words, beyond the fear. Spiritual, a softer guide, no walls to bind, no rules to bide, a journey inward, deep and wide, where soul and universe collide.

It's in the wind, the ocean's roar, in every leaf, in every shore, a truth that speaks in silent breath, of life beyond, of love through death. Religious seeks a path defined, a road well-trod, a clear design, while spiritual flows like a stream, unbound, untamed, a waking dream. One finds God in scripture's word, in ancient texts, in lessons heard, the other feels a force unseen, in every moment, every scene.

Religious kneels before the cross, or prays with beads, with faith embossed, spiritual finds the sacred near, in every heart, in every tear. Both seek the light, both seek the way, to find a truth that does not sway, and though their paths may seem apart, each holds a piece, a sacred part. For In the end, both hearts align, in search of love, in search of the high, religious or spiritual, we seek the same, a quest for peace, we both shall claim.

A God Wink

A gentle breeze, a soft hello, a fleeting sign where love does show. In the quiet moments, swift and slight, a God wink shines like morning light. It's in the laugh you didn't expect, a perfect timing, soul connect. A subtle nudge, a whispered clue, the universe aligning just for you. A butterfly crossing your path by chance, or a song that makes your spirit dance.

The wink of God, so soft, so sweet, a glimpse of heaven at your feet. When doubt clouds over skies of blue, a God wink says, "I'm here with you." In every smile, in every glance, it reminds us there's no such thing as chance. A tender kiss from realms above, a secret sign wrapped up in love.

It says, "You're seen, you're never alone, this journey's yours, but not your own." So when you feel that gentle touch, know it's God's wink, saying much, a quiet gesture, calm and clear, "I'm always with you, ever near.

Chapter VIII:
Love and Connection

The Essence of Love

Love is a whisper in the night, a gentle touch, a softest light, it's in the glance that needs no words, in the silence where hearts are heard. Love is a fire that warms the soul, a guiding star, a gentle goal, it's in the comfort of a friend, a bond that time can never end.

It's in the laughter shared by two, in every "me" that becomes "you," in sacrifices, big and small, in lifting up when others fall. Love is the courage to be true, to stand by someone, to see them through, it's in the tears that cleanse and heal, in the wounds that time may seal.

It's not just found in words or deeds, but in the heart where kindness feeds, in every act that speaks of care, in every dream two souls may share. Love is the thread that weaves us tight, through joy and sorrow, day and night, it's in the hope that never fades, in memories that time invades.

It's in the trust, the steady hand, in walking side by side, we stand, for love is more than just a feeling, it's the core of all true healing. It's patient, kind, and always true, in all the little things we do, a force that binds, that makes us whole, the very essence of the soul.

The Dance of Two

A man and woman, hand in hand, two souls that journey through this land, in love's embrace, they find their way, through night and dawn, through every day. Their hearts, they beat in steady rhyme, through seasons' change, through tests of time, they laugh, they cry, they learn, they grow, in every high, in every low.

At times, they dance in perfect sync, in rhythm's sway, on passion's brink, while other times, they walk alone, each needing space, each needing home. They face the storms that life may send, but find their strength when they defend, the bond they share, both fierce and kind, a love that's patient, love that's blind.

In whispered words or silent gaze, they write their story through the days, a tale of joy, of trials too, of finding self, yet being two. For in the woman's tender heart, the man finds shelter, finds his part, and in the man's strong, steady hand, the woman feels her spirit stand.

Yet more than love, it's trust they build, a quiet peace that's softly filled, with moments small, yet deeply true, a partnership that sees them through. It's in the give, it's in the take, the compromises that they make, for love is not just wild desire, but steady warmth, a constant fire.

So man and woman walk this life, as friends, as lovers, husband, wife, in union strong, in gentle grace, together in this sacred space.

When Cupid Aimed His Arrow

In the realm of hearts, where love's dance sways, I wandered, lost in life's maze. Cupid, with a grin, took aim so true, an arrow of love, through the skies it flew.

Once like a closed bloom, felt the arrow's touch, and love did consume. A dreamer, with hope in his eyes, he found his match in her, to no one's surprise.

Together they stood, as the arrow found its mark, a spark ignited in the day and the dark. Love's sweet surrender, they could not deny,

Under Cupid's watchful gaze from the sky.

So here they are, in love's gentle snare, the both of them a most radiant pair. Struck by an arrow, so potent and narrow, they'll walk side by side, on the path Cupid did hallow.

My Darling Daughter

My darling daughter, light so bright,

You fill my world with purest light,

Your laughter dances in the air,

A song of joy beyond compare. With every step, with every smile, you make the world feel more worthwhile, your curious eyes, your gentle heart, a perfect blend, a work of art. I watch you grow, day by day, in every little thing you say, your dreams take flight, your spirit soars, you open wide so many doors.

The love you give, so full, so true,

Is wrapped in all the things you do,

From smallest glance to softest touch, you've taught me love can mean so much. My heart is yours, forever more, in every laugh, in every chore, through highs and lows, through every tear, I'll hold you close, I'll keep you near.

For you, my darling, are my star,

My greatest gift, just as you are,

And with each moment that we share, I'm grateful just to know you're there. So go, my love, and chase your dreams, no matter how far or wild it seems, I'll always be your biggest cheer, my darling daughter, always near.

The Unspoken Words

Don't wait until the sun has set,

To say the words you won't forget. For time slips by, a fleeting breeze, and moments fade like autumn leaves. The heart beats now, it may not last, tomorrow's sky may come too fast. So take this chance, before it's gone, to tell the ones you love, hold on.

Say "I love you" without delay,

For life can change in just one day. A whisper now, a soul's embrace, can light the dark, can fill the space. For time is fragile, always near, and we can't see what waits in fear. But love outshines the deepest night, a flicker turned to endless light.

So don't hold back, just let it flow, in every word, let loved ones know. For tomorrow's never promised, true…

Today's your chance to say, "I love you."

What Is Love?

What is love but a whispered song,
A force unseen, yet fierce and strong?
A bridge we build from soul to soul,
A path that makes the broken whole.
It's not just words or fleeting bliss,
Not just a touch, a simple kiss.
It's patience when the road grows hard,
A soft embrace, a gentle guard.

It's laughter shared on quiet nights,
A steady hand through life's rough fights.
It's standing close when storms descend,
The kind of bond that doesn't bend.

Love is light when shadows fall,
A voice that answers every call.
A courage born of tender care,
A promise made to always be there.

So what is love? It's all things true—

A gift that grows when shared by two.

A flame that time cannot remove,

A sacred choice, a vow to prove.

Chapter IX:
Growth and Healing

Hope in Healing

In the quiet dawn of a broken day, when the shadows seem too dark to stay, a whisper rises, soft and bright, a glimmer of hope in the fading light. Through wounds unseen and hearts that ache, a promise stirs with each breath we take. For healing blooms in the hardest places, in whispered prayers and tear-streaked faces.

Hope in healing, a fragile spark,

That guides us forward when the world feels dark. It lingers in moments where courage is found, in the silent strength that knows no sound. Though the path is steep and lined with scars, hope dances still beneath the stars.

For every wound, there's a chance to mend, and in the struggle, new beginnings blend. With each small step, the pain recedes, as hope fulfills our deepest needs. In healing's embrace, we come to see,

That hope is the desire that sets us free.

Raise Your Level of Consciousness

Rise above the noise and din,

Where ego fades and truths begin.

Step past the self that craves the lie,

And glimpse the boundless, inner sky.

Leave behind the need to blame,

The cycles of old, the endless game.

Release the weight that holds you bound,

And lift your spirit from the ground.

See the world with open eyes,

Beyond the limits and disguise.

Feel the pulse of something more,

A calling deep from your core.

It's not in wealth, nor pride, nor fear,

But in the stillness, soft and clear.

The path is narrow, yet so wide,

When seen from within, not from outside.

So raise your thoughts, let love unfold,

Embrace the light, both warm and bold.

For higher realms await our quest,

Where soul finds peace, where heart finds rest

Authentic Self

To shed the masks we learn to wear,

The polished fronts, the practiced stare,

Is to uncover what's been veiled,

The self that's raw, unpolished, frail.

It takes a courage fierce and rare,

To strip away, to stand so bare.

To show the world your inner scars,

Your hidden dreams, your deepest bars.

Not molded by what others say,

Not shaped by fears that sway our way,

But bold enough to just be true,

To let the world see all of you.

A freedom flows from being real,

A joy no pretense can conceal.

For in this space, unmasked, you'll find

A peace that quiets every mind.

Be flawed, be bright, be all you are,

A steady light, a blazing star.

For only truth can set you free,

And let your spirit truly be.

Please Help Me Heal

Please help me heal, I'm worn and torn,

From battles fought, from burdens borne.

My heart is tired, my spirit thin,

I've wandered lost, both out and in.

The weight I carry, cold and deep,

It fills my nights, disturbs my sleep.

I've tried to rise, but fear won't part,

It claws and clings within my heart.

So lend a hand, a light, a guide,

To show me hope I thought had died.

Help me find the strength to stand,

To trust again, to reach your hand.

Unravel pain that binds my soul,

Let time and love make pieces whole.

With patience, grace, and warmth that's real,

Please stay with me, please help me heal.

My Inner Child

My inner child, so pure, so free,

A spark of who I used to be.

Hidden deep beneath the years,

Lost in dreams and dried-up tears.

Once bold, once wild, without a care,

With open heart and curious stare.

She danced through life with boundless glee,

Unburdened by what others see.

I hear her voice, a quiet sound,

In moments when no one's around.

A whisper soft, a laugh, a cheer,

A reminder of all I held dear.

I call her back, I let her play,

In fleeting glimpses, day by day.

To heal the wounds, to break the wall,
To feel alive, to risk it all.

My inner child, she leads me home,
Through fields of wonder, skies unknown.
A gentle guide, forever true—
The truest part of me, renewed.

Footprints to Recovery

In the shadows where pain resides, where dreams once fell and hope divides, a path emerges, steady and clear, a journey to healing, step by step, but don't fear.

Footprints in the sand, soft but sure, carving a way where we find the cure.

Guided by hearts, with hands outstretched, a beacon of light when life's been etched.

Each step a promise, each mark a chance, to rise from the ashes, and claim your chance.

With courage in heart and strength in soul, Footprints to recovery will make you whole.

Together we walk, never alone,

Finding a place where love has grown. In every print, a story, a fight, a pathway to peace, from day to night. So, we tread onward, onward still, with hope as our guide and an iron will. Footprints to recovery, brave and true, a journey of healing, for me and you.

Chapter X:
When I Open My Eyes

The Strength in Surrender:

Surrender is not the end of the fight,

Nor is it yielding to endless night,
It's the moment you learn to let go,
To release the weight you no longer know. It's not the fall, it's not retreat,
Surrender doesn't mean defeat.
It's choosing grace instead of strain,
To find the peace beyond the pain. When battles rage inside your heart,
And holding on tears you apart,
There's power in the soft release,
A quiet strength that brings you peace.
For in surrender, truth appears,
Unveiling courage beneath your fears, to lay down arms, to free your mind, Is not to lose, but to unbind. Surrender is a path to heal, to feel what's true, to know what's real,
it's trusting life to take the lead,

And giving up what you don't need.

It's not the end, but a new start,

A way to mend a weary heart,

For letting go creates the space,

To welcome joy, to embrace grace. It's in surrender that we rise,

With open hands, we touch the skies, for in the yielding, we are free,

surrender brings us victory.

The Foundation of H.O.W.

In the journey to heal, to break free, to grow, there are three simple pillars, a path we must know,

Honesty, Open-mindedness, Willingness too, a foundation of strength that will carry you through.

Honesty first, a light in the dark,

It cuts through the shadows, it makes its mark, to face the truth, no matter how deep, to see the wounds, the promises we keep. It's the mirror that we learn to hold,

Reflecting stories we've never told,

In honesty, we shed the lies,

To walk with courage, with clearer eyes.

Open-mindedness follows, soft and wide, a door unlocked, an ego's pride, to learn, to listen, to set aside,

The walls we've built, the need to hide. For in being open, we start to see, that there's more to life than what used to be, new ways of thinking, new ways to cope,

A heart reborn with faith and hope.

And lastly, there's Willingness, the silent key, that opens the door to recovery. It's the choice to change, to rise, to heal, to commit to the journey, the hard and the real. Willingness means we take the leap, to dive into waters that run so deep, to try again, though we may fall, to stand with grace, to give our all. H.O.W., these three, they intertwine, a foundation strong, a steady line, to live with truth, with heart and soul, is to build a life that's truly whole.

Honesty, to face what's real,

Open-mindedness, to learn, to heal,

Willingness, to take each stride,

Together, they become your guide. In recovery's path, they lead the way,

Turning night into a brighter day,

And with each step, as you walk anew, it's the H.O.W. that becomes the strength in you.

No More Drama

No more drama, let it fade,

Like shadows in the evening's shade. Let the noise fall far behind,

seeking peace of heart and mind.

No more battles, no more tears,

leave behind the wasted years.

In the quiet, we reclaim, a life of joy, free from the flame.

No more weight of others' chains,

or holding on to needless pains.

The world is wide, the air is clear,

free to live without the fear.

No more drama, just the balm,

a heart that's healed, a soul is calm.

With every breath, a brand new start, no more drama in my heart.

Is it a Butterfly, a Bird, or an Angel?

Is it a butterfly, soft in flight, with wings aglow in morning light?

It dances freely in the breeze, a whisper floating through the trees.

Or is it a bird that soars on high, tracing arcs across the sky?

With songs of joy it greets the dawn, a messenger, forever drawn.

But could it be an Angel near, with wings unseen, yet always here?

A gentle presence, calm and kind, guiding hearts, easing the mind.

Butterfly, bird, or Angel's grace, each carries love in its embrace.

And though we wonder what we see, they're all a sign of mystery. In fleeting moments, soft and pure, they remind us love will endure.

Whether butterfly, bird, or angel above, They carry the message: we are loved.

Alone in the Universe

Alone in the universe, drifting wide,

Among the stars with none beside.

A silent voyager, small and frail,

In endless night, I set my sail.

Galaxies spin in distant grace,

Yet here I float, a speck in space.

A single soul in vast unknown,

In cosmic silence, all alone.

I gaze at stars that shine and die,

Their ancient light, a whispered sigh.

Are there others who drift like me,

Lost in thought, adrift at sea?

Or am I but a fleeting spark,

A moment bright, then swiftly dark?

Alone, yet bound to all that's near,

In solitude, I face my fear.

For though I wander, lone and free,

The stars still hold a part of me.

Alone, yet not—somehow, I find,

The universe lives in my mind.

Making Peace with One's Past

I've carried the weight, the hurt, the shame,

The broken pieces of my name.

The echoes of mistakes long gone,

Still whispered softly in the dawn.

But now I stand, a little changed,

With eyes that see, a heart unchained.

The past, once sharp, now softens deep,

Like fading scars that learn to sleep.

Wake Up, You're in the Dark

Wake up, you're in the dark, my friend,

Held tight by shadows that pretend.

They whisper lies you've grown to trust,

They feed on doubt, they breed on rust.

Your heart has slept, your eyes are closed,

To endless paths you never chose.

Wrapped in comfort, fear, and ease,

The light obscured by darkened trees.

But there's a world beyond this veil,

A place where dreams can blaze and sail.

Break free from chains that hold you still,

Climb the ridge, ascend the hill.

It's in the courage to let go,

To face what's hidden deep below.

The darkness trembles at the dawn,

For when you wake, it's all but gone.

So open wide your weary eyes,

And see beyond the silent lies.

The world awaits, a spark, a mark—

Wake up, my friend, and leave the dark.

I Have a Voice

I have a voice, strong and clear,

A sound that rises, born from fear.

Once silenced deep, it hid away,

Afraid of what the world might say.

But now it grows, a steady beat,

A flame that rises from defeat.

No longer chained, no longer small,

I stand up tall—I speak, I call.

I have a voice that won't be stilled,

With words of truth my heart is filled.

I'll shout for hope, for love, for light,

For every soul denied their right.

This voice is mine, it's fierce, it's free,

A spark that burns for change to be.

I speak, I sing, I stand, I fight—

My voice, my power, my endless light.

I've learned to hold the hurt with grace,

To give forgiveness space to trace.

The battles fought, the tears I've cried,

No longer hide or haunt inside.

I'm letting go, I'm setting free,

The chains that bound the soul in me.

The past no longer owns my mind,

It's just a chapter left behind.

In peace I find the strength to grow,

To love the lessons life bestows.

For in the quiet, I can see,

That all I've been has set me free.

Redemption

I once was lost, a soul adrift,

Caught in the currents of a rift.

Mistakes I made, and choices wrong,

Echoed loud, a mournful song.

But in the dark, a light did gleam,

A flicker of a distant dream.

A spark of hope, a gentle call,

To rise again, to stand, to fall.

Redemption whispered soft and clear,

A promise held in every tear.

Not perfect, no, but whole once more,

A chance to heal, to close the door.

I've learned to love the scars I bear,

For they are proof that I still care.

The past, a shadow, fades away,

As grace and truth lead me today.

Redemption is a road we walk,

Not just a word, but how we talk.

It's in the kindness we now share,

In every step, in every prayer.

And though I've stumbled on this way,

I rise, I breathe, I choose to stay—

For in redemption's tender light,

I find my peace, I find my fight.

When I Was Young

When I was young, the world was wide,

An endless road, a daring ride.

The days were long, the nights were deep,

With dreams so bold they'd steal my sleep.

Each sunrise brought a brand-new way,

A promise held in light of day.

I chased the wind, I climbed the trees,

I felt my spirit roam so free.

I knew no fear, just boundless sky,

With endless questions, always "Why?"

The world was magic, pure and wild,

Seen through the eyes of a fearless child.

But as I grew, the colors changed,

The world turned calm, a bit estranged.

The spark dimmed low, the questions shrank,

The dreams I held, a weathered plank.

Yet deep inside, that child remains,

Still running through the fields and rains.

A voice that whispers soft and true—

"Remember me, for I am you."

I Was Made From Dirt, What Am I?

I was made from dirt, from earth and clay,

Shaped by hands in a humble way.

Born of soil, the dust, the ground,

In nature's silence, my roots were found.

I feel the sun, I drink the rain,

I know the joy, I know the pain.

My body grows, yet I must yield,

To seasons' turn, to harvest's field.

I am the grass, the trees, the stone,

The pulse of life, the flesh, the bone.

A fleeting breath, yet here I stand,

A work of earth, a mold of sand.

What am I, if not dust and dew?

A spark that fades, but life renewed.

I am the soil, I am the sea—

I am all things, and they are me.

What Is Love?

What is love but a whispered song,

A force unseen, yet fierce and strong?

A bridge we build from soul to soul,

A path that makes the broken whole.

It's not just words or fleeting bliss,

Not just a touch, a simple kiss.

It's patience when the road grows hard,

A soft embrace, a gentle guard.

It's laughter shared on quiet nights,

A steady hand through life's rough fights.

It's standing close when storms descend,

The kind of bond that doesn't bend.

Love is light when shadows fall,

A voice that answers every call.

A courage born of tender care,

A promise made to always be there.

So what is love? It's all things true—

A gift that grows when shared by two.

A flame that time cannot remove,

A sacred choice, a vow to prove

Note to Self

Remember, you're not alone, even when the world feels cold, and unknown.

In moments dark, when doubts arise, look within and see your eyes. you've weathered

storms, you've faced the fight, and found the strength to find the light.

Your worth is more than what you see, you are enough, just as you be. Don't rush to

heal, don't rush to rise, it's okay to feel, to question why.

Take your time, breathe slow and deep, your heart will mend, your soul will keep. You

are a work of grace and fire, built of dreams, and truth, and desire.

So trust yourself, and know the way, you've got the power to seize today. So write this

down and let it stay, a note to you, from you, today, you're worthy, strong, you're loved,

you're true, and every step you take, you grew, and grew, and grew.

Freedom

Freedom is the open sky,

A breeze that whispers, soaring high.

It's breaking chains, it's spreading wings,

It's hearing life's unspoken sings.

It's the courage to speak your truth,

To stand unshaken, brave, and youth.

It's walking paths that none have known,

And carving ways you can call home.

Freedom is the space to dream,

To build your world, to hear your scream.

It's breaking out from all that's told,

To find the beauty, bright and bold.

It's not a gift that's given free,

But earned with hope and dignity.

It's living without fear's tight grip,

And letting go of what can't slip.

True freedom comes when hearts are kind,

When souls are free, when hearts align.

It's not in riches, fame, or gold,

But in the love that makes us whole.

So hold your head, stand tall, and free, and tell me my friend, how free do you want to be.

I Am

I am the whisper of the dawn,

The quiet light that lingers on.

I am the breeze that moves the trees,

The soft embrace of gentle seas.

I am the echo in the night,

A star that twinkles, pure and bright.

I am the mountain, proud and still,

The valley, peaceful, calm, and filled.

I am the song that hearts can hear,

A voice that calls, both far and near.

I am the warmth of sunlit rays,

The fleeting moments of the days.

I am the truth, both raw and clear,

The strength to fight, the hope to steer.

I am the laughter, deep and wild,

The wonder held in every child.

I am the dream that dares to rise,

The silent strength behind the skies.

I am the pulse, the heart, the soul,

A part of all, yet still whole.

I am the journey, long and wide,

The stillness found when I reside.

I am the fire, the endless flame,

The love that calls me by my name.

Blind Faith

Blind faith, a quiet, steady light,

That guides the soul through darkest night.

It asks no proof, it seeks no sign,

But trusts the path, though undefined.

It doesn't need the world to show

The way, the truth, or where to go.

It walks with hope, though eyes may fail,

Believing love will lift the veil.

In stillness, it can find its voice,

A quiet strength, a sacred choice.

It holds the heart when doubts arise,

And carries dreams beyond the skies.

No map, no road, no clear design,

Just whispers soft, a hand divine.

Through storms and winds, it keeps the pace,

A journey built on endless grace.

Blind faith does not demand to see,

For trust alone can set us free.

It's not in knowing every way,

But in the courage to still pray.

So let it lead, this unseen flame,

For in its warmth, we find our name.

Blind faith, a love that cannot fall—

It sees the heart, it knows us all.

9/11: We Will Never Forget

On that day, the sky turned gray,

As shadows fell, we lost our way.

A moment's peace, then shattered sound,

The world stood still, hearts breaking down.

The towers rose, so proud, so tall,

Now fallen, crumbled, after all.

The smoke, the fire, the endless cry,

A nation wept, a thousand sighs.

But from the ashes, strength was born,

A spark of hope that would not mourn.

For in the dust, in fear's embrace,

We found our courage, we found our grace.

Heroes rose with no retreat,

With steady hands and heartbeats beat.

Firefighters, soldiers, all who cared,

They showed the world that love is shared.

We'll never forget the lives we lost,

The families torn, the heavy cost.

But in our hearts, they still remain,

In every tear, in every pain.

We stand together, side by side,

With hope and unity as our guide.

For though the towers may have fallen down,

Their spirit lives in every town.

So let us pledge, with every breath,

To honor those who faced the death.

For in this grief, we'll never part—

9/11 lives within our heart.

We will not forget the skies so wide,

The tears we shed, the hands that tried.

Together, always, we'll rise again—

We are one, through loss and pain.

Dr. Darren C. Skinner: A Journey from Despair to Resilience

Dr. Darren C. Skinner, MSW, Ph.D., is a Bronx-born U.S. Army Veteran, 9/11 survivor, and professional social worker whose personal and professional journey epitomizes transformation, resilience, and the power of self-expression. Growing up in New York City, Darren faced numerous challenges, including struggles with addiction, homelessness, and depression. Despite these adversities, he emerged as a beacon of hope for others battling similar challenges.

Darren's educational journey began with a Bachelor of Professional Studies from the Metropolitan College of New York, followed by a Master of Social Work from Yeshiva University's Wurzweiler School of Social Work. He later achieved the highest academic distinction with a Ph.D. in Social Welfare, solidifying his expertise in the field. His academic accomplishments are not merely milestones but a testament to his perseverance and dedication to personal growth and helping others.

Behind these professional accolades lies a deeply personal story of struggle and redemption. Darren's battle with drug addiction and alcoholism began early in life, leading to moments of darkness and despair. After achieving sobriety in 1989, he experienced a relapse in 2011. However, through the support of addiction treatment programs, a twelve-step recovery process, and his faith, he found renewal and clarity. His recovery journey fueled his desire to inspire others through his work as a clinical Case Manager and Military and First Responder Specialist at Footprints to Recovery.

Darren's passion for poetry began as a child. At just ten years old, he wrote a poem for a school project that won a $25 prize, marking the beginning of his love for creative expression. Though he put writing aside for many years, in 1991, Darren rekindled this passion through a free creative writing class. Over time, poetry became a therapeutic outlet—a way to process and articulate emotions tied to his experiences with trauma, mental health, spirituality, and relationships.

Since 2011, Darren has consistently turned to poetry as a means of self-expression. Initially, his poems were private—a personal journal of emotions, struggles, and reflections. However, his perspective shifted when he shared a poem with a friend in need. Seeing how his words uplifted and inspired others encouraged him to share more of his work, eventually leading to the creation of his poetry collection, From Insanity to Serenity – A Recovering Alcoholic's Journey from Despair to Resilience.

For Darren, writing poetry is not just an art form; it is a spiritual practice rooted in his belief in God's divine providence. He views his ability to write as a grace-filled gift, one that allows him to be authentic and connect with others on a deeply human level. Through his poems, Darren explores themes of spirituality, resilience, mental health, and the human condition.

Darren's life and work serve as a testament to the power of transformation, creativity, and faith. His story resonates with anyone who has faced darkness and found light, offering hope and inspiration to those on their own journeys of healing and recovery.

www.ingramcontent.com/pod-product-compliance
Lightning Source LLC
LaVergne TN
LVHW091536070526
838199LV00001B/84